A Great Family Pet

Nancy Beveridge

ISBN 978-1-64559-577-9 (Paperback)
ISBN 978-1-64559-578-6 (Digital)

Covenant Books, Inc.
11661 Hwy 707
Murrells Inlet, SC 29576
www.covenantbooks.com

To my great-grandchildren
CJ and Calena

Have you ever wanted a pet? Our daughter was eight years old and wanted a pet she could hold. When she was little, she had a goldfish. She felt that she was too old for goldfish. She asked me if she could have a pet that she could actually hold. I thought for a minute and asked, "How about a parakeet?" Aunt Esther bought one for our cousin Larry. They were enjoying the bird.

She asked me where you get a parakeet. I said we could go to Bloomington, the nearest big town ten miles away, and buy one next Saturday.

3

Dad drove us to town on Saturday. When we got to the store that sold parakeets, she found she could choose the color she wanted. There were pretty blue ones, but the chartreuse green birds were so bright and cheery. She picked a chartreuse one.

The sales lady touched the bird on the chest with her finger. The bird climbed on her finger. The sales lady put the bird in a box with ventilation holes. The store had other things we needed. We picked out a cylinder-shaped cage that had one door. We felt it would be easy to clean. Cleaning the cage was going to be our daughter's job. She had time on Saturdays to do it.

The cage had containers for feed and water and also a swing. She still needed bird seed and a cover to put over the cage at night. They also had booklets about parakeets, so she picked one up.

It was evening when we got home. Her father and I helped her set up the cage. Our daughter decided to call her bird "Chippie." After Chippie had a chance to eat and drink, our daughter covered the cage for the night.

The next day was Sunday. When our daughter got up in the morning, she uncovered the cage and checked the seed and water. After church she had time to take Chippie out of the cage. She touched his chest with her finger and he climbed on to it. The clerk at the store told us that all the parakeets had one wing trimmed so they couldn't really fly. Our daughter enjoyed stroking Chippie's head and down his back. He seemed to enjoy it too.

While she did this she would softly say, "Chippie, Chippie, pretty bird," over and over to him. This is what the booklet said to do in order to get the bird to speak.

During the week she would take Chippie out of the cage when she came home from school. It wasn't too many days before Chippie started saying his name, and eventually he said, "Chippie, pretty bird." She put the bird back in his cage while we ate supper and then did her homework.

It wasn't too long before Chippie started climbing up our daughter's sleeve and sitting on her shoulder. He seemed to like her because he got close to her neck and put his head against her cheek. She could watch TV with him sitting on her shoulder.

Sometimes we didn't eat dessert at suppertime and ate it later. One evening it happened to be a dish of ice cream. I dished up three dishes of ice cream and put a dish of ice cream in our daughter's hand. I also gave one to her dad who was nearby, and I had one for myself. Chippie was curious and quickly climbed down her sleeve and sat on the edge of the dish of ice cream. He put his head down to get a beak full of ice cream. He immediately shook his head, sending the ice cream flying everywhere. We all had a good laugh. Chippie went quickly back up her sleeve and sat on her shoulder.

Our daughter and I never saw her Dad take Chippie out of his cage. When school was in session, she went to school in the town where we lived and I headed south to teach at the next school district. That left Chippie alone in an empty house until noon. When Dad came home for lunch, he decided to have Chippie join him. He used some scrap lumber and a dowel stick to construct a perch for Chippie. At the end of the perch, Dad attached a wooden clothespin. He put this stand in a pie pan to catch any bird droppings and potato chip crumbs. When it was time for lunch, Dad put a ruffled potato chip in the clothespin and placed the stand in the middle of the kitchen table. Chippie nibbled on the potato chip while Dad ate his lunch.

When Dad was through, he washed his lunch dishes and our breakfast dishes. One day Chippie either got tired of the perch or wanted to be closer to Dad. He jumped down to the table and then the floor. He made his way over the rug to the back of Dad. Then using his beak and claws, he climbed up to Dad's shoulder, which was quite an achievement considering that Dad was six feet tall. Chippie sat there until Dad finished the dishes. Then Dad put him back in his cage.

Since our daughter came home with her dad late in the afternoon, I was home about an hour earlier and it was usually still light outside. I thought Chippie should get to see more of the outside world. So, I took him out of his cage and put him on the rim of a lampshade near a large window. Chippie would work his way to the edge nearest the window. When I came back to get him, I would say, "Chippie, come over here so I can get you." He seemed to understand because he would work his way around the shade so I could take him off and put him back in his cage. He enjoyed it when I would stroke the back of his head and neck as I walked across the living room.

After a few days, this is what I heard as I walked up to the lamp, "Chippie, come over here so I can get you."

As I said before, cleaning the cage was our daughter's job. She did this on Saturday mornings. When she put Chippie on the back of a chair near the cage, she would tell him he was a "pretty bird." One Saturday the cage was a little messy, so she told him he was a "dirty bird." A couple days later he was saying, "Chippie pretty dirty bird."

We enjoyed Chippie for three years. Then one morning we found his dead body lying at the bottom of his cage. I got a box with a piece of cotton that fit. Dad got the spade and dug a hole in the flower garden. We had a short service and our daughter thanked God for a great pet. I know our whole family missed him. We didn't get another bird because our daughter now had more homework. She wouldn't have had time to really enjoy him. We certainly all have a lot of good memories about "Chippie pretty bird.".

About the Author

Nancy Beveridge is an eighty-five-year-old great grandmother in an assisted living facility. She attended a country grade school. In June of 1955, she graduated from ISNU in Normal, Illinois, with a BS degree. The name of that school changed to ISU. Nancy's first full-time job was teaching home economics in Reed Custer High School in Braidwood, Illinois. After getting married in June of 1956, she became a hospital dietician for a year and a half. Nancy eventually went back to college and took the courses she needed to teach elementary school, which she taught for twenty-three years, eighteen of which she taught fifth grade.

CPSIA information can be obtained
at www.ICGtesting.com
Printed in the USA
LVHW071929010720
659458LV00020B/1249

9 781645 595779